ACTIVITIES FOR BEFORE & AFTER SCHOOL

by
David W. Pratt
Mardi A. Gork

Incentive Publications, Inc.
Nashville, TN

Cover and illustrations by Cheryl Mendenhall
Edited by Sherri Y. Lewis

ISBN 0-86530-211-1

TABLE OF CONTENTS

Introduction 7

ACTIVITY DAYS
Restaurant Day 10
Puppet Day 12
Aeronautics Day 14
Indoor Olympics Day 16
Fashion Show 18
Sandcastle Day 20
Treasure Hunts 22
Great Race Day 24
Make Me Giggle 26
Outdoor Summer Olympics 28

GAMES
Shoe Scramble, Name Game 32
Open Fist, Closed Fist; Telephono; Travelin' 33
Wishing On A Present, Dots, Attributes 34
Slaughter 35
Up, Jenkins! 36
Black Bottom Ball 37
Deck Game 38
Snake In The Grass 39
I Spy 40
Hangman 41
Knots 42
Animal Friends Game 43
Circle Messages 44
Nose Toes 45
Switch 46
Simon Says 47
Kickball 48
Thumb Wrestling 49
Blob Tag 50
What's Missing Or Different 51
Johnny Went To Sleep 52
Flying Saucer Golf 53
Elimination 54
Dodge Ball 55
Paper, Rock, & Scissors 56

CRAFTS

General Materials List...58

Paint...59

    Straw Painting..60

    Tempera Leaf Prints..61

    Watercolor Crayon Resistance 62

Paper Craft 63

    Weaving...64

    Tissue Lamination..65

    Murals 66

Textiles..67

    Ojo de Dios 68

    Paste Batik 69

    Applique 70

Multimedia 71

    Bleach Painting..72

    Mobiles 73

    Diorama...75

    Texture Rubbings...76

    Collage 77

Drawing Materials 78

    Chalk 79

    Crayon Etching 80

CALENDAR ACTIVITIES

January..83

February 84

March...85

April 86

May 87

June 88

July 89

August...90

September..91

October..92

November...93

December 94

INTRODUCTION

ACTIVITY DAYS
This section contains long activities and short activities. These programs are especially useful for full-day child-care, summer, or nonschool days settings. All are energetic, creative, and include all grade levels.

GAMES
A tried and tested collection of unusual games is presented in this chapter. The games are easy to play, do not have a lot of rules, and are quickly taught. Supervision is minimal, and although some require a leader, oftentimes it can be one of the children. The games, grouped by age and ability level, are designed to reduce children's stress in positive ways. They may also be used to extend the curriculum areas of language arts, social studies, and physical education.

CRAFTS
These crafts are for every grade level and can be made from readily accessible materials. Most projects can be completed in one day. This chapter is also an excellent resource for practice in reading, following directions, hand/eye coordination, and large and small muscle development.

CALENDAR ACTIVITIES
Here is a valuable teaching tool to help integrate historical events into the child-care program. Listed in this chapter are over forty activities centered around the calendar months.

RESTAURANT DAY

Children running a restaurant? Why not?

This activity could provide a way to "dress up" that daily snacktime or even provide a vehicle for a full gourmet hot dog and punch meal. Whatever the occasion, there are many reasons for helping children create a restaurant atmosphere. They will gain real-life skills like counting change, food preparation, interior decorating, etc. Bon appetit!

ACADEMIC FOCUS:
– science, health, math, reading

MATERIALS:
– table decorations based on a theme
– construction paper menus
– a variety of snacks
– paper money and/or coins
– table settings (plates, cups, etc.)
– cash register

PERSONNEL:
– hostess
– waiters
– cashier
– "cooks"
– costume designers
– clean-up crew

SETUP:
– table and chairs set for eating area
– cashier register area
– kitchen area with supplies

THE WEEK BEFORE:
–Have children decide on a theme.
   (optional)
– Gather all snacks and serving materials.
– Design and print menus.
– Make table and room decorations to fit theme.
– Reserve room if necessary.

THE DAY BEFORE:
– Prepare snacks if possible.
– Decorate the room.
– Set up kitchen area.
– Practice making change.

SUGGESTED PROCEDURE:
– Customers line up outside.
– Hostess seats customers.
– Waiters take orders and serve.
– Customers eat, then pay bill.
– Clean-up crew cleans tables, etc.

EXTENSION ACTIVITIES:

If you decide to use a theme, it would be a good idea to tie in social studies by making ethnic dishes. "Customers" could then dress in the country's motif.

If possible, sometime try to really cook following a recipe. "Customers" might serve as taste-testers for a competition between classes.

PUPPET DAY

Puppets are a way for both children and adults to enter the magical world of fantasy where dragons still roar and princes still come to rescue fair maidens.

Not only do children enjoy watching a puppet presentation, but they also love to create and produce their own shows. Puppeteering with children can be as elaborate as making marionettes and staging or as simple as using a marker to make a face on the tip of your finger.

ACADEMIC FOCUS:
- literature, language arts, drama, art

MATERIALS:
- finger puppets: paper, markers, tape
- stick puppets: tongue depressors, paper, markers, tape
- sock puppets: old socks, buttons, yarn, thread and needle, fabric
- paper bag puppets: bags, markers, newspaper
- paper-mache: starch, glue, paint, balloons, material, newspaper
- stage and scenery: backdrop or freestanding screens or appliance boxes
- audiovisual equipment (optional)

PERSONNEL:
- puppeteers
- "props" production crew
- announcer
- optional personnel - script writers, music coordinator, lighting and video camera operator

SETUP:

- Reserve room or area to be used (can be classroom, cafeteria, or outside area).
- Station music and announcer away from stage viewing area.
- Videotape should be set close to stage.

TWO WEEKS BEFORE:

- Select stories and assign puppet characters.
- Write script and/or tape narrative.
- Decide if it will be done by the whole class or small groups.
- Assign work teams.

ONE WEEK BEFORE:

- Begin work on scenery, props, or stage setting.
- Reserve performance area.
- Design and print invitation.
- Practice performance.

THE DAY BEFORE:

- Lighting details
- Dress rehearsal

SUGGESTED PROCEDURE:

- Ushers seat audience.
- Announcer introduces the performance.
- After the performance, the announcer introduces the cast and all helpers.

EXTENSION ACTIVITIES:

Using puppets is a great way to encourage children to read important pieces of literature. This also provides great exposure to other cultures and time periods from around the world. Puppets can make the world of literature come alive.

AERONAUTICS DAY

The theme for this day provides a great variety of activities which deal directly or indirectly with flight. This is a day to fly kites, paper airplanes, Frisbees®, parachutes, etc.

ACADEMIC FOCUS:
- science, math, art, social studies

MATERIALS:
- paper
- cloth
- small weights (metal nuts work well)
- straight pins
- felt-tip pens
- crayons
- glue
- balloons

(Materials needed will vary depending on what kind of flight crafts you make.)

PERSONNEL:
- adult administrators (optional)
- group monitors
- lots of aeronauts

SETUP:
- any open area

THE WEEK BEFORE:
- Ask children which projects interest them, and form similar groups for them to work with (e.g., parachutes, paper airplanes, kites, helicopters, pinwheels, balloons, etc.).

- Schedule activity.
- Design posters or "fliers" to promote the activity.
- Ask children to bring materials.

THE DAY BEFORE:
- Gather all materials.
- Plan flight and display contests.
- Make awards.
- Invite other classes to the flights.

SUGGESTED PROCEDURE:
- The day should begin discussing with the children the possible projects they can make and why they should work.
- A major part of the time will be spent completing the projects.
- Schedule "launchings" by type: airplanes, all paper crafts, all gliders, etc. (i.e., 1:30 p.m. parachute drops, etc.).
- Fly creations by classrooms or by type.
- Give awards for longest flight, straightest flight, etc.

EXTENSION ACTIVITIES:
- Give awards for several of the best examples, e.g., originality, etc.
- Display at open house or parents' night.
- Graph distances and compare.

INDOOR OLYMPICS DAY

Is the weather too ugly to go outside? Feeling snowbound with a bad case of group cabin fever? Move tables and chairs out of the way for a day of indoor competition! Most of the summer olympic games can be scaled down with some creativity to be played indoors. An indoor olympic organizing committee of children will get you started as you "go for the gold" on this day.

ACADEMIC FOCUS:
- physical education
- math
- measurement

MATERIALS:
- balloons
- straws
- paper plates
- yardsticks
- ribbons
- markers
- beach balls
- "soft" balls (those made "safe" to use in the house)
- opening and closing banners, etc.

PERSONNEL:
- judges for each event
- team captains
- announcer, timekeeper, record keeper

SETUP:
- any large, empty room

THE WEEK BEFORE:
- Plan activities and their locations.
- Set up teams and team captains.
- Advertise event with posters or notes home.
- Organize opening and closing ceremonies.

– Order or make ribbons and trophies.
– Make flags for countries represented.

THE DAY BEFORE:
– Gather ribbons and trophies.
– Verify children's job responsibilities.
– Designate and label areas for each event.
– Take time to discuss the philosophy behind the Olympic games and elements of good sportsmanship.

SUGGESTED PROCEDURE:
– Begin opening ceremonies with fanfare.
– Parade all judges and participants around school.
– Suggested events:

TRACK AND FIELD EVENTS:
  Shot Put – Use balloons in place of the shot.
  Javelin – Use straws in place of the javelin.
  Discus – Use paper plates in place of discus.
  Standing Broad Jump – Have children place toes on the line and jump.
SOCCER:
  Soccer with a foam ball.
WRESTLING:
  Thumb wrestling (be sure to paint faces on the thumbs).
VOLLEYBALL:
  Play on knees with either a balloon or a beach ball.

– Be sure to award participation ribbons or certificates to all the children.
– Keep a positive attitude for competing at any level.
– Have closing ceremonies.

EXTENSION ACTIVITIES:
Many types of events can be modified along this theme. You may want to design obstacle courses of various ability levels, or use your own creative imagination to design other skills.

Use this as a springboard for studies of other countries or the history behind the Olympics.

This could provide interest in a fitness program to improve abilities and to go back and break those old records.

FASHION SHOW

Do you ever wonder what to do with leftover lost and found clothing or how to get older children involved in role playing? This activity gives you the way to solve those problems and will be a guaranteed "fun-raiser." Although most of your time will be spent preparing for the show, you will be richly rewarded as you watch your kids while they are "puttin' on the ritz."

ACADEMIC FOCUS:
- careers
- social awareness
- following directions
- describing
- organizational skills
- design elements

MATERIALS:
- old or new clothes
- long tables for the walkway
- microphone
- record player
- background music
- assorted accessories
- models
- video camera

PERSONNEL:
- dresser
- models
- sound person
- emcee
- video camera operator

SETUP:
- Put long tables end-to-end as a runway.
- Have a small step up to tables (box or chair).

– Seat audience around tables.
– Place emcee at the front of tables.
– Put record player and sound person at one side of tables.

THE WEEK BEFORE:

– Schedule room and equipment early to avoid conflicts.
– Design and distribute posters to advertise event.
– Decide on a theme, e.g., winter, summer, outrageous designs, etc.

THE DAY BEFORE:

– Have dress rehearsal with all the "cast" and crew.
– Keep activity moving.
– Keep time moving.
– Be certain everyone knows his/her responsibilities.
– Make copies of programs for distribution.

SUGGESTED PROCEDURE:

– Prepare a written list of models in order of appearance.
– Prepare a short description for each outfit.
– Models appear one at a time or in small groups.
– Emcee reads description while models display outfits.
– Audience claps or responds accordingly.
– Models are backstage or behind curtain to help with changing.
– Introduce models after the show.
– Rewind the videotape for the kids and have a good laugh.

EXTENSION ACTIVITIES:

This can be done by grade level and then presented to other grades. Each grade can have its own theme. You might want to invite parents, too. This could even be used as a fund-raiser. Art can be integrated by having children pose to be sketched.

Also, the history and development of fashion trends can be discussed. Creative writing could be used to describe the students' favorite outfits and why they liked them.

SANDCASTLE DAY

This is a day for young artists and architects alike. Sandcastle building encourages children to use both their large and small muscles and also encourages their design abilities. Today is the day children can get dirty and have fun at the same time.

ACADEMIC FOCUS:
- tactile representations
- special awareness
- math volume, quantity, balance
- art form, design, texture
- architectural elements

MATERIAL:
- sand or sand areas
- water, hoses
- "tools" such as rakes, containers, spoons, etc.
- awards

PERSONNEL:
- construction crews
- older children as team leaders
- architects
- judges panel

SETUP:
- outside sand area and/or playground
- rope or string to designate team areas

THE WEEK BEFORE:

- Announce construction plans.
- Allow children to form teams.
- Preview photos to form teams.
- Talk about design possibilities.
- Choose a design theme (optional).

THE DAY BEFORE:

- Have tools collected and available.
- Sketch designs (optional).

SUGGESTED PROCEDURE:

- Thoroughly soak sand 2 hours ahead.
- Saturate again 1 hour ahead.
- Assign areas and teams.
- Pass out "tools."
- Set time limit.

UPON COMPLETION OF ACTIVITY:

- Offer guided tours of each piece of property.
- Judges give awards for various categories (originality, funniest, etc.).
- Give a participation award to all.
- Allow time for destructing creations.

EXTENSION ACTIVITIES:

This activity could be used to construct a city as a social studies lesson. Use math to construct all buildings, etc., to scale.

On a larger theme, try constructing a castle, farmlands, houses, or a model of your own city.

TREASURE HUNTS

Can you imagine finding a "real" treasure map of the property with an "X" on it to mark the spot where the pirates buried their loot?

Treasure hunts often begin with a mixture of fact and legend. This mood will set the stage for this exciting activity. The thrill of the hunt will be almost as much fun as finding the "treasure."

ACADEMIC FOCUS:
- geography and map skills
- reading
- logic
- critical thinking
- history

MATERIALS:
- treasures
- maps (made by children, you, or a committee)
- clues (visible or written)
- large area to work within

PERSONNEL:
- map-makers and designers
- helpers (to hide treasure and/or mark clues)

THE WEEK BEFORE:
- Introduce maps and how to read them.
- Read *Treasure Island* by Robert L. Stevenson or a similar treasure story.

- Play games or have students write papers requiring them to follow directions on their own.
- Decide how to make treasure maps and who will hide the treasures.
- Decide how children will hunt for treasure (clues, riddles, maps, etc.).

THE DAY BEFORE:
- Choose helpers (these will not hunt for treasure).
- Assign partners.
- Designate a time limit.

SUGGESTED PROCEDURE:
- Draw a map and let children follow it to hidden treasure.
- Cut the map into pieces, and hunt for the map and then the treasure (optional).
- Follow colored tapes, arrows, or anything that will get you there.
- Hide lots of different treasures and send many small groups.
- Make it a lesson in map-making and direction-finding.

EXTENSION ACTIVITIES:
Try making some of the different types of maps such as population, rainfall, topographical, physical, etc. Encourage competition by keeping a record of time elapsed before finding the treasure.

GREAT RACE DAY

This is a day of competition! Children will compete against the clock, their fellow students, or maybe even against the staff. Realizing that too much competition can be destructive, it is important on this day to include races in which all can be winners.

You can have running races, walking races, crawling races, hopping races, mind races, bicycle races, relays, obstacle courses, cleaning up the room races, etc. Emphasize that all are winners who try.

ACADEMIC FOCUS:
- P.E. skills
- math
- social development skills
- good sportsmanship

MATERIALS:
- stopwatches
- prizes
- participation ribbons (optional, but nice)
- measuring tape
- chalk (if needed to mark tracks)
- racing equipment (trikes, scooters, skates, etc.)
- microphone to announce each event
- cones (optional) to mark tracks or obstacle course

PERSONNEL:
- timers for each event (optional)
- line judges
- announcer

- helpers
- medical person (on-call basis)
- recorders

SETUP:
- a race area (large or small)
- some inside areas and some outside areas
- start/finish lines and specific courses

THE WEEK BEFORE:
- Decide upon agenda and types of races.
- Pick location(s).
- Make chart to record winners.
- Choose announcers and judges.
- Design and make invitations or announcements.
- Design award certificates.
- Order ribbons (optional).
- Discuss rules and good sportsmanship.

THE DAY BEFORE:
- Be prepared, enthusiastic, and patient.
- Congratulate **ALL** participants.
- Keep events running on time.
- Be cautious of injuries.
- Remind children that all participants are winners.
- Encourage a variety of races.
- Match participants by age.

EXTENSION ACTIVITIES:
Discuss major races (car, running, etc.). Maps of tracks can be drawn and studied.

MAKE ME GIGGLE

Children in today's hurried society sometimes don't spend enough time being silly and enjoying childlike humor. This activity will help you set up a "game show" with judges, guest comedians, and contestants.

ACADEMIC FOCUS:
- health
- history
- social studies
- language arts

MATERIAL:
- stopwatch
- chairs
- recorder (optional)
- microphone (optional)
- room to hold event
- posters or other advertisers

PERSONNEL:
- three person panel (one adult to help judge)
- timer
- lots of very funny kids
- emcee

SETUP:
- Reserve room able to hold the audience and staging area.
- Set up stage area (table for comedians, table for judges, stool for contestant).
- Set up microphone and sound system (optional).
- Set chairs in rows for audience.

THE WEEK BEFORE:
- Discuss with children what is classified as funny today.

- Discuss what is good humor and what is off-color.
- Learn terms for funny dialogues such as gags, one-liners, etc.
- Define "stand-up comedian."
- Design invitations and/or posters announcing event.

THE DAY BEFORE:

- Confirm room setup and seating for guests.
- Arrange for refreshments (optional).
- Practice telling jokes or making each other laugh.

SUGGESTED PROCEDURE:

- Set up a game show format with emcee.
- Contestants are chosen at random from the audience.
- Contestants must sit in the front of the audience.
- Each contestant must remain straight-faced for 30 seconds while the panel tries to make the contestant laugh or giggle.
- Each contestant gets three 30 second rounds.
- Finalists move into six 30 second rounds.
- Rotate panel participants.

SUGGESTED PROCEDURE:

Learn why a person laughs and what happens physiologically when we laugh. Research different comedians and their delivery styles. Imitate some of the comedic styles. Introduce props as a way to enhance comedy. You may want to award "Best Of Show" or other types of awards.

OUTDOOR SUMMER OLYMPICS

In this activity there is something for everyone to do even if he/she chooses not to compete.

All of the positive values we see demonstrated during the Olympics, i.e., sportsmanship, friendship, cooperation, etc., can be demonstrated and taught through an activity like this one. Be sure to highlight the winners, encourage all who competed, and thank those who helped.

ACADEMIC FOCUS:
- physical ability and agility
- good sportsmanship and social skills
- math
- science

MATERIALS:
- sand area
- baton for marathon relay race
- paper on wall area (for high jump)
- balls – soccer, volleyball
- awards
- participation ribbons (optional)
- microphone

PERSONNEL:
- judges for each event
- timers
- announcer (optional)
- scorekeepers
- first-aid station monitors
- setup and teardown helpers

SETUP:

- Map out the field area to be used.
- Note the location of each event.
- Set start/finish lines.
- Post record-keeping area.

THE WEEK BEFORE:

- Decide which events will be held.
- Set up teams and "countries."
- Advertise the event with posters and fliers.
- Plan opening and closing ceremonies.
- Make or purchase awards.
- Make flags for the countries represented.

THE DAY BEFORE:

- Verify everyone's responsibilities.
- Set up for opening, closing, and award ceremonies.
- Discuss winning, losing, and good sportsmanship.

SUGGESTED PROCEDURE:

- Begin with opening ceremony – you may want to pattern it after the real Olympics and use music and flags, or just keep it simple.
- Run events simultaneously by type – all track and field in the morning and all ball games in the afternoon, for example.
- Remember to allow rest and provide lots to drink.

– Suggested events:
    Track and Field events:
        Dashes – 40 yds., timed.
        Long Jump – into sandy area, measure with yardstick or tape measure.
        Marathon – Who can do the most laps in 15 minutes?
        Relay Race – baton pass between 4 or 6 people.
        High Jump – post a piece of paper on the wall; jump and place the highest mark on the paper.
        Soccer – shortened field and time limit; single elimination.
        Volleyball – use a beach ball and play a regular game.
        Wrestling
– Have closing ceremonies and awards presentation.

EXTENSION ACTIVITIES:

It might be interesting to let the different teams represent actual countries when competing. Students could make the flags, and it would make a nice opening and closing. Study the maps for location of these countries and maybe even introduce snacks from them as well.

30

GAMES

SHOE SCRAMBLE

GRADE LEVEL: GRADES K-5

DIRECTIONS:

Everyone removes their shoes and places them in a pile in the center of the room. The winner of the game is the first team to:

- have their own shoes on and tied
- have someone else's shoes on
- have any shoes on
- have two different shoes on
- put shoes on other people
- find their shoes while blindfolded

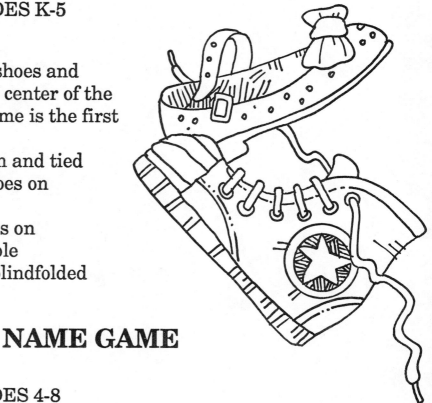

NAME GAME

GRADE LEVEL: GRADES 4-8

DIRECTIONS:

Everyone sits in a circle. The starting player states his/her name and then adds something which begins with the same letter. Some examples include Dave - doughnuts, John - jelly, etc. To make this more interesting, try introducing categories such as foods, animals, fictional characters, and many more. The game continues around the circle with each player repeating all that was said and adding his/her name to the list.

OPEN FIST, CLOSED FIST

GRADE LEVEL: GRADES 2-6

DIRECTIONS:

Each child needs a partner for the game. The designated partner makes a tightly clenched fist. The other partner should try to pry open this fist within 30 seconds. Try keeping track of winners and losers. Encourage competition by moving winners up and losers down on a chart.

TELEPHONO

GRADE LEVEL: GRADES 2-6

DIRECTIONS:

A minimum of five children work best at this game, more if you have them. Conduct the game in whispers. The first child starts the game with a short message and whispers it into the ear of the next person. This message is relayed from one student to another until it reaches the last person. The last person must orally repeat what he/she heard. Usually it is a whole different message. To make it interesting, try using tongue twisters or alliterated sentences and see what develops! This is a good method of reinforcing listening skills among the children.

TRAVELIN'

GRADE LEVEL: GRADES 3-6

DIRECTIONS:

This is another excellent game for practicing listening skills as well as letter sounds. Start with the children in a circle if possible. The beginning child should state, "I'm going to Alaska and I'm bringing an alligator." The next child must repeat what was just said and then proceed in the same manner with the next consecutive letter in the alphabet. The game continues in this way until all the letters of the alphabet have been used. If a child cannot remember, he/she loses the turn and is passed over until the next time around.

A variation of this game is to play using alliterative sentences. For example, "Donald Duck drove to Disneyland, and he took a dollar." (This style of playing will work well with older children.)

WISHING ON A PRESENT

GRADE LEVEL: GRADES K-4

DIRECTIONS:

Since it is often difficult to encourage children to open up about themselves or their desires, this is a game that will do just that in a nonthreatening way. The teacher or care-giver brings a wrapped present to the room. It can be any size and wrapped in any type of paper, either thematic or generic. Each child then takes a turn imagining what might be in the box, either for themselves or for others.

Two extensions of this activity include drawing what might be in the box or writing a story about what is inside.

DOTS

GRADE LEVEL: GRADES 3-6

DIRECTIONS:

Development of critical thinking skills plays an important part in this game. The players may be organized into small or large groups, or even into a whole group. The playing area is a field of dots set in a square pattern. An average game is about 20 by 20 dots. Each player may connect two dots by drawing a line (no diagonal lines). The object of the game is to be the last player to enclose a square and initial it. Each square closed allows the player another turn. The player with the most initialed squares is the winner. One idea to save the care-giver some time is to construct the playing field of dots, laminate it, and play with water soluble markers. This way, a board can last several seasons.

ATTRIBUTES

GRADE LEVEL: GRADES 2-6

DIRECTIONS:

A board is covered with three different shapes in three different colors and three different sizes with a lot of space between each one (for example, large yellow squares, medium green squares, and small blue squares, etc.). The students are allowed seven questions (as a whole class) to determine which shape, size, and color the care-giver has selected. Questions can only be answered by the care-giver with a "yes" or "no." The winner then becomes the one to select a shape and take questions. If no one can guess, the game begins once more. Again, this is excellent for developing critical thinking skills.

SLAUGHTER

GRADE LEVEL: GRADES 3-8

MATERIALS:

– parachute
– 2 Frisbees™
– 2 "flat" balls

LOCATION:

– carpeted inside or grassy outside
(needs to be large enough area to spread parachute)

DESCRIPTION:

This is a rough, tough game, and children must be warned upfront that they will get bumped and banged. The parachute is spread out on the ground. Two small teams are chosen, and everyone removes their shoes. Players must keep hands and knees on the parachute at all times. Each team has a ball and a Frisbee™. The Frisbee™ is turned upside down and becomes the goal. The Frisbees™ and balls must also remain in contact with the parachute. The purpose of the game is to take your ball and put it in the other team's Frisbee™. You also must prevent the other team from doing the same. Body contact, taking the other team's ball, sitting on your Frisbee™ are all okay, etc. Winning team must make 5 goals.

VARIATION:

While the game is in play, all body parts must be on the parachute. If a player is forced to have any body contact outside the parachute, he/she is removed from the game until the next goal is scored.

UP, JENKINS!

GRADE LEVEL: GRADES 2-8

MATERIALS:

– one to three large coins
– 6 - 8 foot table and a chair

LOCATION:

inside or outside

DESCRIPTION:

Have six to eight children sit around a table, and the person who is "It" stands at the end of the table. When "It" says," Go," he/she should turn his/her back to the table while those seated at the table place their hands underneath it and begin passing the coins from hand to hand. "It" allows this to continue for about 1 minute, then turns to the group and says, "Up, Jenkins!"

In unison, the group around the table makes fists with their hands and brings them to the tabletop. Again in unison, the group chants "1,2,3!" and on "1" and "2," the group hits their fist to the table, but on "3" everyone slaps their hands to the table, palm down. The coins will now be hidden under someone's palm, and "It" has two guesses to locate the coins. If "It" can locate the coins, the person holding the coins becomes "It." If "It" cannot find the coins, he/she continues to be "It," and the play is repeated.

BLACK BOTTOM BALL

GRADE LEVEL: GRADES 2-6

MATERIALS:

- "flat" soccer or volleyball
- 4 orange traffic cones

LOCATION:

- large open room, preferably uncarpeted

DESCRIPTION:

BLACK BOTTOM BALL is a soccer variation. Children are divided into two teams – side and end boundaries are set up and discussed. Shoes are removed. Children must kick, push, or slide the ball with their feet (or legs) and try to score a goal just as in soccer. All players must keep their bottom in contact with the floor. Locomotion is achieved by using feet and hands to scoot along the floor. The goalie can use hands, but his/her bottom must maintain contact with the floor, also.

VARIATION:

Use more than one ball at the same time to create an interesting twist.

DECK GAME

GRADE LEVEL: GRADES K-8

MATERIALS:

- 2 ropes, string, or other ways of making lines

LOCATION:

- large open area, inside or out

DESCRIPTION:

Divide the playing area into thirds and designate each area with a letter, number, or color. All players should start in the center area. The leader will then call out one of the names of the other two areas. Children all run to the called area. The last child to cross the line is removed from the game. The leader continues to call out locations, and the children run from area to area. Each time, the last one to cross is eliminated. The winner is the last child in.

VARIATION:

The leader can try to fool older children by calling one area while pointing to another or by calling the same area in which the children are already standing.

SNAKE IN THE GRASS

GRADE LEVEL: GRADES K-3

MATERIALS:

– none

LOCATION:

–large open area, inside
  or out

DESCRIPTION:

SNAKE is a tag game. All participants start standing up inside the boundaries. "It" becomes a snake and must crawl on his/her belly, using feet and hands. Anyone touched is "bitten" and must instantly fall down and turn into another snake. The play continues until everyone has been turned into snakes. The last person touched will be the first snake for the next game. (Note: If played outside, clothes could get dirty.)

VARIATION:

Different animals and their means of locomotion could be substituted (e.g., elephants, monkeys, fish, etc.) Try calling the game "Babies in the Grass" and have the children crawl when touched.

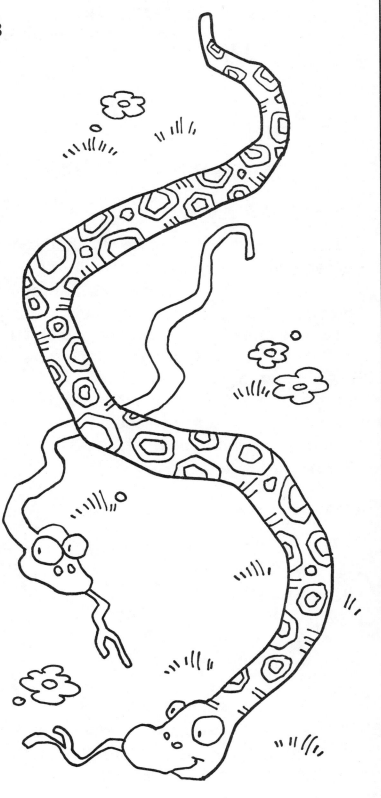

I SPY

GRADE LEVEL: GRADES K-1 (with adult help)
2-6 (moderate supervision)

MATERIALS:

– none

LOCATION:

– large open area, inside or outside (inside is best)

DESCRIPTION:

I SPY is a variation of an old child's game called "20 Questions." "It" is chosen from among the group playing. "It" then selects an object that is in plain view of the rest of the group. Play begins when "It" says, "I spy something in this room." Members of the group are allowed to ask questions one by one about the object. "It" can only answer with a "yes" or "no" response. Anyone can make a guess as to what the object is, but if he/she is wrong, he/she is out of the game. Whenever someone in the group guesses the object, he/she becomes the next "It," and play begins once more.

VARIATION:

The objects used for guessing may be predetermined or written on slips of paper. "It" will select a piece of paper and must play that object, or you may want to limit the number of questions allowed (such as 10, 15, etc.) as in the game "Attributes," page 34, where students are only allowed 7 questions in all. Participants may not make a guess until all the desired questions have been answered.

HANGMAN

GRADE LEVEL: GRADES K-8 (depending on the prereading skills of the K class)

MATERIALS:

- pencil and paper, or
- marker and poster board, or
- chalk and chalkboard

LOCATION:

- inside (usually)

DESCRIPTION:

HANGMAN is a word guessing game. The object is to guess the mystery word before getting "hung." One person selects a word, and without saying it out loud then marks the playing board with a series of short lines, one for each letter of the word. Off to one side, a small gallows is drawn, also. Then one at a time, children guess various letters of the alphabet. If the letter is part of the mystery word, it is put into the proper line(s) in the word. If the letter guessed is not part of the mystery word, it is written below the gallows, and a body part is added to the hangman rope. "Hanging" (losing) is completed when enough incorrect letters have been guessed to complete the entire stick figure body. The winner guesses correctly and discovers the mystery word before the entire figure is drawn in the gallows.

VARIATION:

Use teams to play. Let each team have its own "gallows" and compete for best times. Try using phrases or more obscure words.

KNOTS

GRADE LEVEL: GRADES 3-8

MATERIALS:

– none

LOCATION:

– inside or outside
  (carpet or grass is best, with no furniture)

DESCRIPTION:

KNOTS is a cooperative game in which a small group of children try to untangle a mess to the best of their ability. Groups of 4, 6, or 8 players stand in a circle facing each other shoulder to shoulder. Each player takes his/her right hand, extends it, and grabs someone else's right hand across the circle. The same is done with the left hand **except** that players may not take hold of any other player's two hands. They must be connected to two different players at once. The group is then "tied up in knots," and cooperation is now essential to become untangled. Players may not release hands but must bend, dip, reach, stretch, and do whatever it takes so they eventually find themselves standing hand in hand in a circle.

ANIMAL FRIENDS GAME

GRADE LEVEL: GRADES K-2

MATERIALS:

– none

LOCATION:

– wide open space, inside or outside

DESCRIPTION:

This is a role-play game in which children can act and sound like various animals. The object is to find an animal the same. The children are placed in a large area and must be at least 2 steps away from each other. The leader of the game will walk to each and whisper in his/her ear what animal he/she should be. When the leader signals the play to begin, children should walk, act, and make noises like the animal they have been assigned. When they find someone who acts the same, they group together and find more of the same animal.

VARIATIONS:

Older children could play this game blindfolded and find each other by sound only. Children could draw names of animals instead of being assigned an animal. Animal classifications could be used: mammals, fish, birds, reptiles, etc.

CIRCLE MESSAGES

GRADE LEVEL: GRADES K-6

MATERIALS:

– none

LOCATION:

– inside or outside

DESCRIPTION:

CIRCLE MESSAGES is a game of verbal communication skills and great laughs over mix-ups. The object of the game is to pass along a verbal message from person to person around in a circle by whispering, then seeing how the message changes at the end of the circle..

Have the class sit in a circle shoulder to shoulder. The leader of the group thinks of a message to pass around. The message should be funny or out of the ordinary. The leader begins play by whispering the message to the first person who then repeats the message to the next player, and on around the circle. The last person will repeat the message aloud just as he/she perceives it to be, then compares it to the original message.

NOSE TOES

GRADE LEVEL: GRADES K-8

MATERIALS:

– none

LOCATION:

– inside or outside

DESCRIPTION:

NOSE TOES is a game of word tomfoolery. The object is to confuse your opponents enough so they slip up and make a mistake.

Make a circle with the group of participating players. One person decides to go first and then turns to the next person. The first player points to one part of his/her body and names a different part. For example, a player might point to his/her nose and say, "This is my elbow." The second player turns to the third player and points to the same body part but again assigns it an incorrect name. When a player makes a mistake, he/she is eliminated from the circle. The game continues until only one player is left.

VARIATIONS:

Play with a partner and develop a system of scoring points to make the other player mess up.

SWITCH

GRADE LEVEL: GRADES 1-6

MATERIALS:

- lines painted on the ground for 4-square or
- chalk to make 4 corners and centerpoint

LOCATION:

- outside on a hard surface

DESCRIPTION:

SWITCH is a game of quick maneuvers and fast feet. The object of the game is for three pairs of players to trade positions before "It" can steal their corner from them.

Begin play with 4 players standing on the four corners of the square (approximately 10' x 10', or the size of a 4-square playing area). "It" stands in the center of the square. When "It" says, "Go!" the players try to switch positions before "It" can steal their corner. Possession of a corner is accomplished by covering the exact mark for the corner with your shoes. If three sets of players can switch positions before "It" can steal a corner, "It" is out, and another "It" is selected. If "It" is able to steal a corner away from a player, then that player is out, and "It" takes his/her position on the square.

SIMON SAYS

GRADE LEVEL: GRADES K-2

MATERIALS:

– none

LOCATION:

– inside or outside

DESCRIPTION:

SIMON SAYS is a verbal game of following directions. The object is to do exactly what Simon says to do and nothing else. Choose Simon from the group, or the teacher/leader can be Simon. Simon tries to trick the players into making a mistake.

The play begins when Simon says, "Simon says...," followed by a set of directions. For example, "Simon says stand up." Or, "Simon says touch your nose." All players should follow exactly any directions preceded by the words "Simon says." Occasionally, Simon may try to trick the group by issuing a direction without saying "Simon says" first. Any player who mistakenly follows these directions is eliminated from the game. The winner is the last player remaining in the game.

VARIATIONS:

Every player gets five tickets or tokens initially and may use them to pay for any mistake during the game. This way, players are eliminated only when after making a mistake, they have no more tickets or tokens left.

KICKBALL

GRADE LEVEL: GRADES 2-6

MATERIALS:

– soccer or kickball
– 4 bases

LOCATION:

– outside playground play area

DESCRIPTION:

KICKBALL is similar to baseball except that players kick a ball instead of hitting a ball with a bat. The object is to be the team with the most runs scored at the end of the game.

The players are divided into two teams, and bases are set like a baseball diamond. One team is chosen to kick first, and the other team begins out in the field. The pitcher rolls the ball on the ground to the first person kicking. That person kicks the ball and runs to the first base. Players are "out" if the ball can be thrown to the baseman before the runner touches the base or if they are tagged with the ball below the waist before they get to the base. Each team gets three outs, foul balls are played over (be sure to define the foul-ball area first), and runs are scored for those whose players are able to make it around the diamond touching all the bases, returning to home base without being tagged.

VARIATIONS:

Older children can kick with the opposite leg they usually kick with. PARTNER KICKBALL is played when 2 players hold hands throughout the entire game.

48

THUMB WRESTLING

GRADE LEVEL: GRADES 1-6

MATERIALS:

– none

LOCATION:

– inside or outside

DESCRIPTION:

THUMB WRESTLING is a game that tests superior thumb strength and dexterity. The object is to pin down your opponent's thumb with yours.

Play begins by choosing your opponent. The players then reach across a table and clasp their fingers together with thumbs pointed up and free to maneuver. Players bow their thumbs three times while counting out loud together. At the count of three, the wrestling begins. A winner is declared when one player is able to hold down the opponent's thumb for 3 seconds or more without raising his/her hand off the table.

VARIATIONS:

Thumbs can be decorated for this event. Hold tournaments and graph results.

BLOB TAG

GRADE LEVEL: GRADES 1-6

MATERIALS:

– none

LOCATION:

– large outside area with well-defined boundaries

DESCRIPTION:

BLOB is a tag game in which the blob continues to grow in size. The object is to be on the run and not to be eaten by the blob.

Define the boundaries before beginning play. Anyone who goes outside the boundaries must automatically join the blob. One person is chosen (or volunteers) to be "It" and begins by chasing people and trying to tag them. When a person is tagged, he/she is absorbed by the blob. They must hold hands and continue to chase and tag people. When the blob grows in size to 4 players, then the blob can split into two blobs of 2 people each. Play then continues with 2 blobs, then 3 blobs, etc. The winner is the last person to be absorbed into the blob, and this will also be the person to start the next game.

WHAT'S MISSING OR DIFFERENT?

GRADE LEVEL: GRADES K-4

MATERIALS:

– tray or table to display items
– 8-12 small miscellaneous items

LOCATION:

– any room (classroom size)

DESCRIPTION:

WHAT'S MISSING OR DIFFERENT? sharpens a child's powers of observation, memorization, and recall. The object is to decide what has been changed about a particular group of items.

A child is chosen to be "It." The teacher/leader gathers the 8-12 items and puts them on the table or tray for display. Each child is given 30-45 seconds to study and memorize the lineup. The child then closes his/her eyes or leaves the room while another child removes an item from the lineup. "It" then views the items again and answers the question, "What is missing or different?"

VARIATIONS:

This game can be played with teams of players scoring points for their team with correct answers.

Older children might want to switch more than one item or not remove any at all. They might even change the order of objects instead.

JOHNNY WENT TO SLEEP

GRADE LEVEL: GRADES 1-3

MATERIALS:

  – none

LOCATION:

  – inside in an open space

DESCRIPTION:

    JOHNNY WENT TO SLEEP is a great game to let children be silly, follow a leader, and become flexible.

    Organize the group in a circle and decide on a person to start. The first person says, "Johnny went to sleep and he slept like this." That person demonstrates how Johnny went to sleep by waving arms, shrugging shoulders, head bobbing, etc. The next person again says, "Johnny went to sleep and he slept like this." He/she adds another body motion to the previous one. Each successive person adds a body movement. When everyone gets too silly, start a new game.

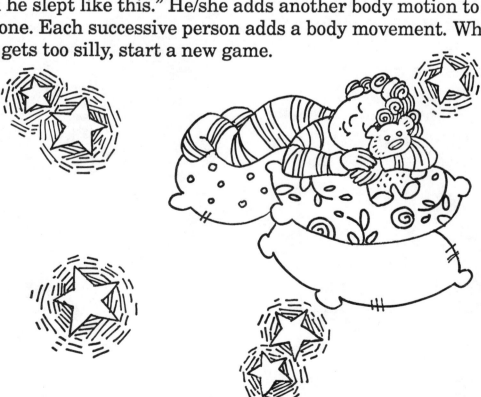

FLYING SAUCER GOLF

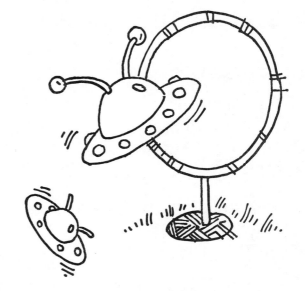

GRADE LEVEL: GRADES 3-8

MATERIALS:

- one flying disk for each player
- score sheets and pencils (1 for every group of four children)
- Hula-Hoops® (holes), or some other "target" to throw toward

LOCATION:

- large, outdoor play area

DESCRIPTION:

FLYING SAUCER GOLF is similar to regular golf except instead of hitting a ball into a hole, you throw a disk to hit a target.

If a large group plays, divide into groups of four players each and designate a person to keep score in each group, or a fifth nonplayer might want to keep score rather than play and act as a caddy for the group. Hand out score sheets and pencils. On the score sheets, list the hole numbers, locations, and par (average) for that hole. Before playing, make sure everyone knows where the holes are and their order. Play begins with the first foursome "teeing" off. Groups must decide in what order they will throw, and they must maintain this order until each person hits the target. Every throw of the disk counts as one stroke. At the end of each hole, count the number of throws it took to hit the target. The scorekeeper then records this score. At the end at the game (usually 9 holes), the scorekeeper totals the strokes for each person. The lowest scorer is the winner.

VARIATIONS:

- Make flags with numbers on them to designate holes.
- Use a smaller course and throw the disk with your opposite hand.
- Give a handicap (bonus) to the younger children before playing.
- Have playoffs and tournaments.

ELIMINATION

GRADE LEVEL: GRADES 3-8

MATERIALS:

- tennis ball
- a "ball wall"

LOCATION:

- outside, play against a tall wall or side of building

DESCRIPTION:

ELIMINATION is a fast-paced catch and throw game. The object is twofold: 1) do not fumble the ball when catching it, and 2) get the other people "out."

At least three people should start the game. The first person throws the tennis ball against the wall. As it comes rolling or bouncing back, someone else attempts to pick it up with one hand. If the ball is picked up successfully, then that person returns the throw to the wall and the play goes on. However, if the player fumbles the ball, the ball must be immediately dropped and the player must run to tag the wall. Any other player may then pick up the ball and throw it at the wall. If the ball touches the wall before the first player reaches it, then he/she is eliminated from play. If he/she beats the ball to the wall, then he/she can rejoin the game. The winner is the last person to remain in the game.

DODGE BALL

GRADE LEVEL: GRADES K-6

MATERIALS:

  – one rubber playground ball
  – designated playing area (painted circle works well)
  – hard surface area

LOCATION:

  – outside playing area or inside gym

DESCRIPTION:

The object of the game is to throw the ball and hit someone to get him/her out of the game, avoid being hit by the ball, and be the last person in the game (winner).

A basic game of DODGE BALL begins by placing everyone except for two throwers inside a designated playing area. These children begin to throw the ball and try to hit other children inside the designated area below the waist. If a player inside the area is hit by the ball, then he/she must move out of the area until the last person is left. He/she is then the winner.

VARIATIONS:

  • Players who catch the ball without dropping it remain in the circle.
  • Instead of a designated circle, players line up against a wall.
  • Players have to hop on one foot, and throwers must roll the ball.

PAPER, ROCK, & SCISSORS

GRADE LEVEL: GRADES 1-6

MATERIALS:

– none

LOCATION:

– inside or outside

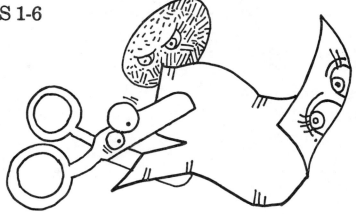

DESCRIPTION:

This basic game is played by 2 people who sit facing each other. They make one hand into a fist and the other is left open, palm up. At the same time, both players hit their fists into the open hand 3 times and count "1, 2, 3!" On "3," each player "shows" either paper (shown by a flat palm), rocks (shown by making a fist), or scissors (shown by making a cutting motion with fingers). Winners are determined as follows: paper covers rocks, rocks break scissors, and scissors cut paper. If both players show the same object, that is a tie and there is no score. The first player who wins 10 games is the winner.

VARIATIONS:

This can be played as a team tag game. Two teams are created, and after a quick huddle to determine which object the whole team will use, they stand face-to-face at a center line. In unison everyone says, "1, 2, 3!" and shows his/her object. If it is a tie, nothing happens. If two different objects are shown, losers try to retreat to the "safe" zone before being tagged by the other team's players. If they are tagged, they must join the other team; then play starts again.

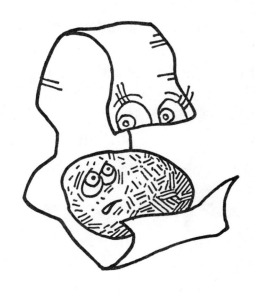

CRAFTS

GENERAL MATERIALS LIST

ADHESIVES:
- white glue
- paste
- rubber cement
- tape (all types)
- spray adhesive (optional)
- glue gun (optional)

SCISSORS:
- left and right handed
- blunt tipped for smaller children
- pinking shears (optional)

RULERS
(and other measuring devices)

STAPLES and STAPLERS

SINK and WATER

WORKTABLES
(with washable surfaces)

DISPLAY AREA(S):
- tables or wall
- general area
- individual room areas

CONTAINERS:
- various sizes for: water, paste, paint, starch, etc.

PAPER CUTTER

PINS and TACKS

CLEANING MATERIALS:
- sponges
- paper towels
- all-purpose cleaner
- razor blades

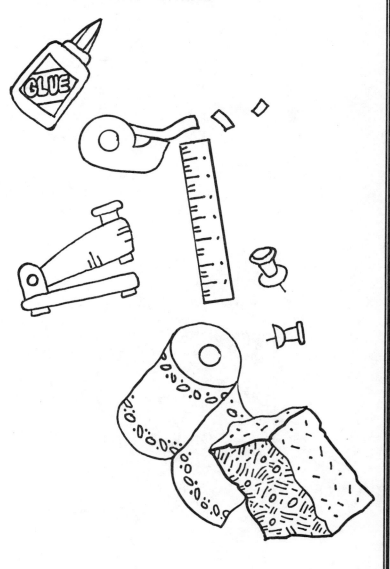

PAINT

In addition to paint as a basis for art projects, consider the ability to use it in teaching color theory. Let children experience how colors blend to form new colors. You may want to introduce a unit on paint with some color-blending experiments. Talk about primary colors (red, yellow, blue) and secondary colors (green, orange, purple). Show the children a color wheel. Let them use paint to color in an open-ended activity, stressing the experimental aspect.

Beginning exposure to the medium of paint is best done starting with finger paint, then tempera, acrylic, and finally watercolor.

Paint can be applied with fingers or brushes or from one surface onto another as in simple printing.

- **STRAW PAINTING**

- **TEMPERA LEAF PRINTS**

- **WATERCOLOR CRAYON RESISTANCE**

STRAW PAINTING

ACADEMIC FOCUS:
- art (line, shape)
- science (seasons, nature)

TIME FRAME: 1-2 hours

MATERIALS:
- construction paper (white, blue, black, etc.)
- straws cut in half
- tempera paint
- tissue paper (optional)

PROCEDURE:
- Pass out construction paper and put names on it.
- Water down tempera paint color(s) of choice.
- Place blob of paint on paper – use dropper.
- Carefully blow paint in one direction with straw forming lines.

HELPFUL HINTS:

Younger children may enjoy this experience without having to make anything concrete. Just let them blow the paint using different colors to make a free-form design. Later you can examine their creations for evidences of wide or narrow lines, curved or straight lines, etc.

Older children can extend this activity by making tree trunks and branches with the paint and adding details according to the seasonal changes with tissue paper. You may want to use this activity in conjunction with Johnny Appleseed Day.

TEMPERA LEAF PRINTS

ACADEMIC FOCUS:
- science and nature
- art (color theory, simple printing)

TIME FRAME: 1-2 hours

MATERIALS:
- various types of heavy veined leaves
- construction paper for background
- tempera paint in styrofoam meat trays
- newspaper to cover work area (or oilcloth)
- smocks (optional)

PROCEDURE:
- To keep leaves fresh, pick on the day of the activity.
- Cover work area and put on smocks.
- Pass out construction paper and put names on it.
- Pour paint into trays.
- Dip leaves into paint (one leaf per color, veined side down).
- Gently press veined side of leaf onto paper and lift.
- Overlap leaf prints in a random manner.
- Dry, frame, and display.

HELPFUL HINTS:

You can do a lot to teach color theory with this activity. Try using "warm" colors (red, orange, yellow), or "cool" colors (blue, violet), or neutrals (white prints on black construction paper) for a different effect.

Let students examine the veins in the leaves prior to painting, and take time to discuss their functions.

WATERCOLOR CRAYON RESISTANCE

ACADEMIC FOCUS:
- science
- language arts (resist, wash)
- elements of design
- math (proportion, depth)

TIME FRAME: 2 hours

MATERIALS: (depending on theme)
- construction paper background (white)
- watercolors and brushes
- crayons
- newspaper to cover work area (optional)
- smocks (optional)

PROCEDURE:
- Pass out construction paper and have children put their names on it.
- Let children draw their picture (theme or no theme).
- Make a light wash of watercolor over top of the crayon (see below).
- Let dry and display.

HELPFUL HINTS:

Be sure to have the children fill in areas completely and to press hard!

Some suggested themes are: space (use a black wash), the ocean (a blue wash), or Halloween (a black wash).

Keep the brush strokes in one direction only with a watered down amount of watercolor for best results.

PAPER CRAFT

Another very versatile medium is paper. You can cut, fold, twist, tear, or build with paper. Each type of paper, such as construction, tissue, crepe, etc., has individual properties and can be used in a wide variety of projects. Be sure to keep a good supply of types in a wide range of colors.

Teach children to conserve paper by cutting close to the edge and to save scraps for future three-dimensional projects, or as fillers. Also, when pasting, instruct children to be conservative. Using these techniques will allow your program budget to stretch and teach children to value their resources.

- **WEAVING**

- **TISSUE LAMINATION**

- **MURALS**

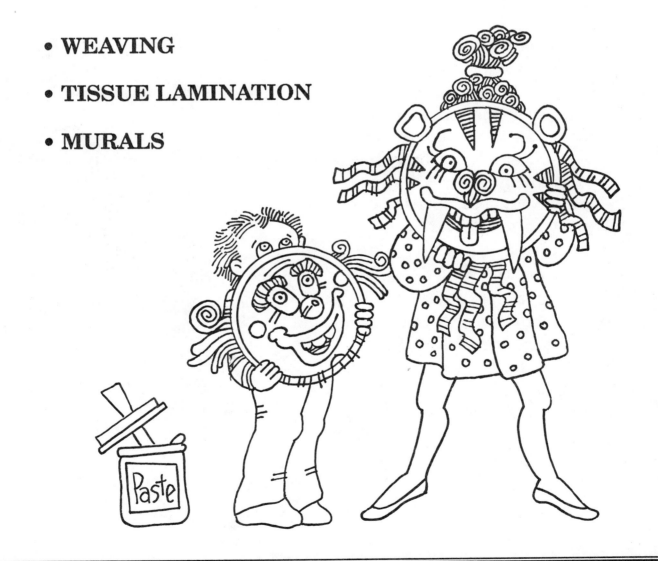

WEAVING

(Also see TEXTILES on page 67.)

ACADEMIC FOCUS:

– math (pattern and pattern extension)
– language ("over," "under," and other descriptive words)
– seasonal art activities (holiday themes)

TIME FRAME: 45 minutes-2 hours

MATERIALS:

– construction paper in various colors cut into strips with paper cutter
– glue or paste (optional)
– crayons (optional)
– additional material to decorate (optional)

PROCEDURE:

– After securing strips of paper, model for the students the over-and-under technique used in weaving.
– When complete, edges may be glued to keep secure.

HELPFUL HINTS:

Place mats are a good introduction to this procedure since they are square. Other shapes include hearts, Christmas trees, etc.

When students can master the single over/under technique, allow them to extend this activity by doing combinations their own way – 2 over, 1 under, etc.

TISSUE LAMINATION

ACADEMIC FOCUS:
- science (themes like the ocean or space)
- art (colors, overlap, shape)
- social studies (time periods or eras)

TIME FRAME: 1-3 days

MATERIALS:
- newspaper to cover work area
- paintbrushes
- tissue paper, cut or torn
- construction paper
- water

PROCEDURE:
- Cover work area (optional).
- Mix starch in water (1 part water to 3 parts starch).
- Generously fill brush with starch and apply to construction paper in a small area.
- Carefully place tissue on wet area; try not to wrinkle.
- Overlap tissue.
- Brush on top with a small amount of starch if necessary to remove wrinkles.

HELPFUL HINTS:

Use a limited amount of tissue colors for best effect. For example, use blue for the sky and green for the ground as a background. Then take construction paper and cut out buildings and/or trees and glue on top of dried laminations. Dinosaurs are a good topic for this activity because the children can fashion volcanoes out of construction paper as well as dinosaurs and other details.

Lamination can be used as a background medium in projects such as murals, dioramas, or pictures.

You may want to frame them because lamination has a tendency to curl once dried. A strip of construction paper at the top and bottom will also help control the curl.

MURALS

ACADEMIC FOCUS:
- social studies (communities)
- science (environments, seasons, habitats, etc.)
- history (great moments of, eras)
- art (design elements, composition, transition, repetition of pattern)

TIME FRAME: 1-3 hours

MATERIALS:

- butcher paper background
- construction paper
- felt-tipped markers
- paint/crayons/chalk/charcoal/etc.
- tissue paper and starch (for possible lamination)
- glue, scissors, pencils
- display area

PROCEDURE:
- Decide on the theme and possibilities.
- Divide group into committees, each responsible for one component in the mural, i.e., transportation, buildings, people, etc.
- Allow for time to construct, paint, or draw.
- Assemble by committee beginning with background and ending with detail work.
- Display proudly!

HELPFUL HINTS:
Murals can facilitate many kinds of lessons. An historical mural reinforces learned material. A community mural can be used as an alternate map activity. The possibilities are limitless. Also, a mural made from the outline of various students' profiles creates an interesting backdrop to a classroom. Use murals for extensions of lessons or for art's sake itself. Either way it's a hit!

TEXTILES

Textiles are exciting to work with because of the endless varieties available and because they surround children in everyday life. Most of the textiles used in classes can be donated by the students themselves. In this way, children will transfer the learning from a classroom situation into their real world, making the learning more meaningful.

It is a good idea when working with textiles to take time to discuss the origin of the material with the class before beginning a project. Many children (and adults) are unaware that cotton actually comes from a plant or that wool must be spun even today. This information will be exciting for the children to learn.

If possible, try to let the class dye their own fibers for a project. This can be a good science investigation.

By allowing students to satisfy their own natural curiosity about textiles, a possible career choice could be in the making.

- **OJO DE DIOS**

- **PASTE BATIK**

- **APPLIQUE**

OJO de DIOS

ACADEMIC FOCUS:
- art (form and design)
- math (symmetry)

TIME FRAME: 1-3 hours (depending on size and complexity)

MATERIALS:
- yarn in various colors
- white glue (optional)
- tongue depressors
- optional finishing decorations, e.g., feathers, beads, etc.

PROCEDURE:
- Tie tongue depressors (one on top of the other) together at center.
- Twist sticks 90° to form cross shape.
- Pick colors of yarn.
- Beginning at center with color number one, weave yarn around stick once.
- Continue until sticks are covered.
- Begin next color the same way.
- Continue until sticks are covered.
- For finishing, knot last yarn loop on backside.
- Attach tassels, feathers, beads, etc., to ends of sticks.
- Put name on back with masking tape.

HELPFUL HINTS:

Use these in small versions to make mobiles, or try stacking them one on top of another. You can also try making multiples by using more than one cross piece and twisting around gradually. You might like to investigate card or loom weaving as an alternate type of weaving. Older classes may enjoy dyeing their yarn, also.

PASTE BATIK

ACADEMIC FOCUS:
- language arts (batik, resist)
- art (color)

TIME FRAME: 2 days

MATERIALS:
- batik paste: 1/2 cup flour, 1/2 cup water, 2 teaspoons alum, blended well
- material squares (10" x 10" for each child, or smaller)
- squeeze bottles (1 for each small group of children)
- cold water fabric dyes in a variety of colors
- containers of dye colors
- brushes
- wax paper
- smocks (optional)
- blender
- strainer

PROCEDURE:
- Make batik paste.
- Set theme for projects such as animals, nature, etc.
- Allow children to draw design making sure they fill the material space.
- Place fabric on wax paper.
- Use squeeze bottle filled with batik paste to "draw" picture outlines.
- Allow to dry completely.
- Keeping wax paper under fabric, paint spaces of picture with fabric dye colors. (Children may need to wear smocks at this point.)
- Allow to dry completely.
- Finish by rubbing or scraping the paste off the fabric. (This can be messy.)
- Iron out wrinkles.
- Mount on construction paper with rubber cement (optional).

HELPFUL HINTS:
The yield for this recipe is only enough for three 10" x 10" designs, so adjust accordingly. When blending, make sure there are no lumps or they will clog the squeeze bottle opening. Keep designs simple for best results. Also, try stitching designs together to make a drapery for the reading center!

APPLIQUE

ACADEMIC FOCUS:
  – art (design reproduction, stitchery technique, shape)

TIME FRAME: 1-3 days

MATERIALS:
  – fabric scraps
  – yarn, thread, string, etc.,
    and needles big enough to
    carry the material used
  – material backing
  – drawing materials
  – batting for stuffing

PROCEDURE:
  – Have children sketch their design.
  – Reproduce design elements with fabric.
  – Stitch fabric shapes in position on fabric backing, leaving
    a small opening.
  – Stuff batting into opened area. Stitch opening to secure batting.
  – Make decorative overlay stitches to finish (optional).
  – Display.

HELPFUL HINTS:

  Obviously this is designed for older children. Projects may be as simple as a small quilt or as complicated as a scene from a window. It is not necessary to fill all the appliqued areas with batting. In fact, you may not want to fill any at all and concentrate on just reproducing the picture in fabric. Overlay stitches are another optional item. This looks good on quilts, place mats, etc., but only as a small interest area in still lifes or scenes. Finished projects look nicest when hung from a dowel or when framed.

MULTIMEDIA

The term "multimedia" means just that — a variety of mediums used in one particular project. In some ways, these projects are less confining because they allow for students' artistic interpretation through several mediums. It is easy, however, to go beyond the creative and into the chaotic if too many mediums are introduced at the same time. To avoid this, be sure that students are generally familiar with a majority of articles to be used, and introduce the newer ones with a short time set aside for experimentation. Take time to fully explain the procedure for a multimedia project with careful attention to the order in which mediums are to be used.

- **BLEACH PAINTING**

- **MOBILES**

- **DIORAMA**

- **TEXTURE RUBBING**

- **COLLAGE**

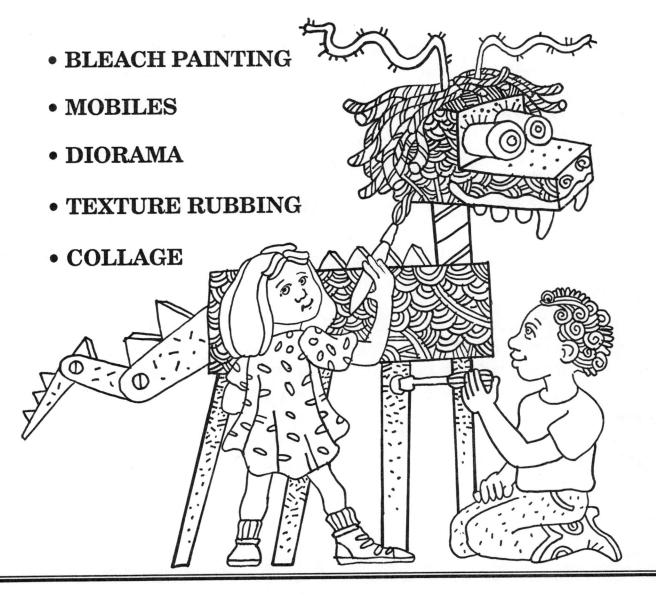

BLEACH PAINTING

ACADEMIC FOCUS:
- science (colors, chemical reactions and changes)
- art (shape and design, detailing)
- language arts (if used as a springboard for a short narrative on what happens)

TIME FRAME: 1 hour

MATERIALS:
- construction paper (brown and dark blue work well; others are not as good.)
- cotton swabs for each child
- bleach in containers
- crayons (for detailing)

PROCEDURE:
- Have children sketch their picture onto the construction paper lightly using a pencil or chalk.
- Dip cotton swab into bleach and use it to "color" area(s) within the picture.
- After finishing all bleached areas, add finishing details with crayon.

HELPFUL HINTS:

The children should be amazed at the color changes that take place from using the bleach. This is one of the reasons it will make a good writing activity later. Sometimes the construction paper will not turn any color except white, so you may want to experiment ahead of time to achieve the desired results with the children. Discuss "details" and how much it enhances the finished work. This may lead to further experiments in color exchanging using solar graphics or markers on wet construction paper as future projects.

MOBILES

ACADEMIC FOCUS:
- math (balance, size, weight)
- science (unique materials used)
- art (form, spatial awareness, symmetry)

TIME FRAME: 1-2 days

MATERIALS:
- main suspension frame (sticks, dowels, branches, etc.)
- string or yarn to suspend sections
- thematic materials
- glue or paste (optional)

PROCEDURE:
- Decide upon theme.
- If using natural materials, arrange them from largest to smallest first.
- Estimate different weights of materials.
- Experiment to see which elements will balance.
- Assemble and hang.

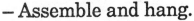

HELPFUL HINTS:

Mobiles that are pleasing to look at as an art form in itself are the easiest to make for younger grades. Older children can handle more direction. Let them use the mobile to show what one might find in the ocean, for example. The lowest section of the mobile would display what might be on the bottom of the ocean; next section what might be found at a shallower depth, and so on, until the surface where boats, waves, and the sun would be found. Be sure to include the perception of color change as the depth decreases. This is one of the many examples of projects which can be incorporated into a mobile.

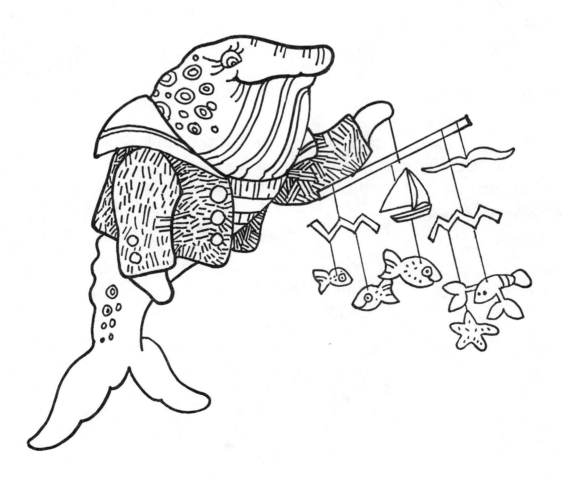

DIORAMA

ACADEMIC FOCUS:
- science (themes, habitats)
- art (proportion, depth perception)
- social studies (communities, eras in time)

TIME FRAME: 3 days-1 week

MATERIALS:
- shoe boxes, boards, or even paper as a base
- paints
- construction paper
- figurines (optional)
- crayons
- glitter
- tissue paper
- miscellaneous items, depending on theme

PROCEDURE:
- Decide on theme or moment in time.
- Discuss layout, design, and proportion (closer objects appear larger).
- Paint or color back of shoe box or base material.
- Assemble and display.

HELPFUL HINTS:

A diorama can have a theme, or it can just show a moment in time. It is important to spend some time discussing with the children what they want to accomplish. One project for older children would be to have small groups each construct a section from a larger construction. For example, each group could make one of a number of rooms in a castle which could be put together as a larger display later.

TEXTURE RUBBINGS

ACADEMIC FOCUS:
- art (texture, design)
- science (observation, recording data)
- language arts (tactile, surface)

TIME FRAME: 1 hour-1 day

MATERIALS:
- thin paper for backing
- crayons, pencils, charcoal, chalk
- objects displaying a raised surface

PROCEDURE:
- Discuss the terms "tactile" and "texture."
- Decide upon type of rubbing.
    1. LEAF - Use various leaves done in fall colors.
    2. NATURE - Take a nature hike and accumulate rubbings from various natural materials found along the way.
    3. ENVIRONMENT - Rubbings from within a defined environment or room.
    4. ARTIFICIAL - Created templates from which to take a rubbing and create a pattern design.
- Place paper over the object and rub gently with the side of the crayon, etc.
- Set a time limit.
- Let children create and display proudly.

HELPFUL HINTS:

Even younger children will enjoy this activity if you make it a little more structured. By dividing the paper by folding or making a large scribble design first, children can fill in each area using a different color for each space.

Older children may enjoy making random designs in this activity.

COLLAGE

ACADEMIC FOCUS:
- art elements such as texture, pattern, and design
- organizational skills for thematic collages
- balance and proportion for still-life collages
- science for natural collages

TIME FRAME: 2 hours-2 days

MATERIALS:
- wallpaper
- magazines
- fabric
- paper scraps
- used greeting cards
- just about anything else

PROCEDURE:
- Decide upon type of collage
  1. Experiential - Made just for the experience.
  2. Thematic - All materials reflect a certain era or theme such as the 1940s or roses.
  3. Still life - Made from an original sketch. Various materials are pieced together. Make a projected time frame to help structure the activity.

DRAWING MATERIALS

There are any number of drawing materials readily available with an equal number of projects to match. Before starting any particular project, allow children to experience the properties of the drawing material designed for that particular lesson. Ask the children to experiment and find out how the materials react to pressure, shading, overlapping, drawing on wet surfaces, etc. Make lines and connect them to make shapes. Ask them what this material does best. Even if you have no specific project in mind, allow children to try different drawing materials.

- **CHALK**

- **CRAYON ETCHING**

CHALK

ACADEMIC FOCUS:
- math (shapes, pattern)
- art (design, color, negative and positive printing, overlap)

TIME FRAME: 45 minutes

MATERIALS:
- shape templates of a circle, square, etc.
- chalk in various colors
- black construction paper

PROCEDURE:
- Pass out paper and have children put their names on it.
- Distribute colored chalk (either put a group of colors in a container at each group of children, or allow them all to share).
- Pass out templates.
- Instruct children to hold template on paper and make outward strokes using the chalk.
- Start at the center of the shape and stroke outward and onto the paper. The result is a negative print.
- Have the children use different shapes and different colors to create the design.
- Encourage them to overlap their shapes.

HELPFUL HINTS:

After the children have experienced negative prints, use the cutout shape to incorporate some positive prints into their designs. To extend this activity, the children can use construction paper and make more positive and negative shape designs.

CRAYON ETCHING

ACADEMIC FOCUS:

– art (etchings, design, color, shape)

TIME FRAME: 45 minutes-1 hour

MATERIALS:

– white construction paper
– crayons
– material for matting or framing (optional)

PROCEDURE:

– Have children create a rainbow, random design, or multicolors on paper.
– Fill space with colored crayons.
– Completely cover picture with black crayon.
– Use paper clips or blunt scissors to etch a picture or design by scraping away the black and exposing the colors beneath.

HELPFUL HINTS:

Be sure the children understand that they must press their hardest on both of the crayon applications for best results. It is not necessary for them to position the under colors to accommodate the etched design on top. The most interesting effect is when there is little or no relationship to the position of colors underneath and the finished picture.

Have the children plan what they will etch before they actually begin so they have a good idea ahead of time.

CALENDAR ACTIVITIES

JANUARY

HIGHLIGHTS:
 1.....New Year's Day; Betsy Ross born, 1752
 2.....Louis Braille born, 1809
 6.....Carl Sandberg born, 1808
14.....Albert Schweitzer born, 1875
15.....Martin Luther King born, 1929
17.....Benjamin Franklin born, 1706
18.....Muhammad Ali born, 1942
30 ....Franklin D. Roosevelt born, 1882

EVENTS:

NEW YEAR'S PARTY – Celebrate the new year uniquely by concentrating on "new." Plan ahead with a "new" theme. Have participants bring a new word to class and try guessing correct definitions, or make up pretend ones! Wear a new outfit, learn a new game, or try a new recipe together. Learn something new by discovering how the months got their names from the Roman gods' names.

CELEBRATE LOUIS BRAILLE'S birthday with an introduction to the Braille alphabet. Have children practice writing their names in Braille dots, and then using a blunt pencil, push on the dots. This will create a raised surface on the back of the paper, much the same as the Braille typewriter creates. Or, if you can, try bringing a Braille typewriter for the children to try. Expand this unit by including more of the senses, discuss handicaps, or have a lesson centered on just sight, vision, or optical illusions.

BENJAMIN FRANKLIN not only discovered electricity and many other fascinating things, he also designed the first glass harmonica. This instrument originally was made of a series of glass disks partly submerged into a column of water. The disks are rubbed by an extending arm to produce sounds. This ethereal sound can be reproduced in the classroom by filling up glasses with different levels of water and using a dampened finger to run around the rim of the glass to produce a tone. Try matching a few pitches with the piano and playing a simple tune. Explore sound creation in other ways, too.

FEBRUARY

HIGHLIGHTS:

2.....Groundhog Day
7.....Laura Ingalls Wilder born, 1867
11.....Thomas Edison born, 1847
12.....Abraham Lincoln born, 1809
14.....St. Valentine's Day
15.....Susan B. Anthony born, 1820
22 ....George Washington born, 1732

EVENTS:

GROUNDHOG DAY shadows are fun to draw on the playground. Have children take turns tracing each other's shadow. Repeat this procedure and change chalk colors every hour. Measure and plot the shadow as it grows and moves on a chart. Expand into a discussion of shadows and how they are produced. Read the poem *My Shadow* by Robert L. Stevenson. Try developing a shadow play from a favorite song.

SHADOW PLAY day can be an extension of the Groundhog Day activities. Students select a favorite poem or song to illustrate and record it for later use. Draw all characters onto tagboard (only the outline needs to be drawn). The characters are cut out; then very thin dowels are attached at the bottom. Scenery pieces are optional. The stage can be as simple or as complex as you want. Essentially, it needs to be a square-shaped frame (a cardboard box works well) with a white paper front (butcher paper is fine). A light is directed from behind onto the paper. The tagboard puppet characters are placed onto the white paper, again from behind, creating a shadow for the viewer. The presentation of the characters then follows along the plot as the recorded version is played. You may want to share some of the historical background for this particular art form with the class as well.

VALENTINE'S DAY – the AIMS Educational Foundation has a great activity using conversation hearts to teach math and science concepts while having fun. Use the hearts to sort, classify by color, graph, and use as a basis for number sentences and simple addition and subtraction problems.

MARCH

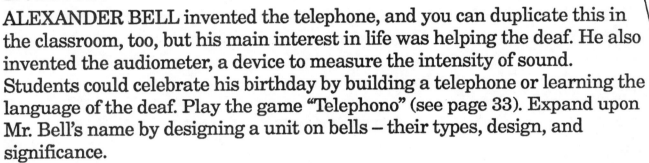

HIGHLIGHTS:

2 .....Texas Independence from Mexico, 1836
3 .....Alexander Graham Bell born, 1847
14 .....Cotton Gin invented by
      Eli Whitney in 1869
17 .....St. Patrick's Day
18 .....Robert Frost born, 1874
21 .....First day of spring

EVENTS:

ALEXANDER BELL invented the telephone, and you can duplicate this in the classroom, too, but his main interest in life was helping the deaf. He also invented the audiometer, a device to measure the intensity of sound. Students could celebrate his birthday by building a telephone or learning the language of the deaf. Play the game "Telephono" (see page 33). Expand upon Mr. Bell's name by designing a unit on bells – their types, design, and significance.

KITES – Try buying three different types of kites, and make your own kites ("Aeronautics Day," page 14). Show them to the class and ask students to predict which will fly best. Graph the predictions making either a bar or picture graph. Then take the kites out and fly them. Discuss the predictions/results.

MANY CHILDREN HAVE LEARNED ABOUT ELI WHITNEY'S COTTON GIN, but most are unaware that cotton is actually a plant. After discussing Mr. Whitney's contribution to science, talk about how plants give us a variety of products. See if children can identify room items as being organic or nonorganic. This would even make a good interactive bulletin board.

WHEN TALKING ABOUT ST. PATRICK'S DAY, be sure to include a short discussion about Ireland and its important crop, potatoes. Have one potato for every group of 2-3 children. Let them count and record the number of eyes, weigh them using any standard of measurement you have handy (blocks, unifix cubes, tiles, etc.), measure and record the circumference, have potato races using the potato rolled with a spoon, and finally, carve a design on half the potato and make prints after inking.

APRIL

HIGHLIGHTS:

  1.....April Fool's Day
  2.....Hans Christian Andersen born, 1805
  3.....Pony Express Service began, 1860
12.....Civil War started, 1861
23.....William Shakesphere born, 1564
26.....John James Audubon born, 1785
27.....Samuel Morse born, 1791

EVENTS:

EVERYONE KNOWS APRIL SHOWERS BRING MAY FLOWERS, so take time to talk about showers. Begin with clouds. Familiarize students with the cloud names: cumulus, cumulonimbus, cirrus, stratus, etc. Make cloud pictures using cotton. Finish with water erosion and its effects.

WHEN CELEBRATING MR. AUDUBON'S BIRTHDAY, begin a study about birds. Learn how birds are a class of animals. Their wings make them unique to their class, and hollow bones help them fly. Discuss how all birds do not fly (penguins and ostriches). Different birds need different habitats — let children try drawing some or making a diorama. Observe and name birds native to your area or state. Do you have a state bird?

SAMUEL MORSE developed the morse code as a means of communication. Learn some simple dot and dash patterns, or illustrate on a chart the patterns for each alphabet letter. This makes a nice class project. Then, try sending some messages. This could begin a mini-unit on methods of communication. Remember Mr. Bell? What other types of communication are there (flags, signal lights, singing, writing, talking, etc.)?

MAY

HIGHLIGHTS:

5 .....Children's Day in Japan
9 .....Mother's Day became public holiday, 1914
20 .....Amelia Earhart began first solo flight, 1932
21 .....Charles Lindbergh finished first transatlantic solo flight, 1927
30 .....Memorial Day first observed, 1868

EVENTS:

ALTHOUGH MAY 5 IS OFTEN REMEMBERED AS CINCO de MAYO, try celebrating Children's Day as an alternative. In this festival, flags in the shape of a carp are flown for each boy. (Have girls pick out a fish shape for their flag as well.) Fish are used here because Japan's fishing industry is one of the largest in the world. Discuss fish, following the example of the discussion about birds from April, and describe differences between fish and birds. Do a crayon resistance drawing of an aquarium scene. Let children use crayons, pressed down heavily while drawing, to draw fish and plants on construction paper as they would appear on the inside of an aquarium. Let children draw with a brush dipped in watercolor paint across the picture of fish and plants (see "Watercolor Crayon Resistance," page 62) to create the effect of water.

COMBINE AMELIA EARHART'S SOLO FLIGHT AND CHARLES LINDBERGH'S TRANSATLANTIC FLIGHT into a special day by discussing air travel today. Design airplanes or hot air balloons and fly them (see "Aeronautics Day," page 14). Graph the distances flown as a class project.

MAY TRADITIONALLY IS A MONTH FOR FLOWERS. Create a paper-mache model of the inside of a flower. Discuss the function of the parts of flowers. Try growing some flowers in the classroom. Experiment with regulating various amounts of light and water, and record the results. Measure growth and chart it daily. Let students research to find out the names of the various state flowers.

JUNE

HIGHLIGHTS:

8 ...Ice cream first sold, 1786

14 ...Continental Congress adopted the flag, 1777

15 ...Benjamin Franklin proves lightning is a form of electricity

16 ....Valentina Tereshkova, first woman to orbit the earth, 1963

17 ....Helen Keller born, 1880

EVENTS:

WHEN ICE CREAM WAS FIRST SOLD on June 8, it began a whole new industry for the United Sates. Ask students to bring hand-cranked ice cream makers, and make some ice cream together. Find out the ingredients in ice cream and how it changes to form the ice cream itself. Have you tasted astronaut's ice cream? You can get a sample of it from a science museum in your area. It's fun to experience because even though it's not cold, it still tastes like real ice cream. Have a taste treat and try some in the class.

BE SURE TO TALK ABOUT VALENTINA TERESHKOVA, the first woman to orbit the earth. Talk about the planets (be sure to play G. Holts's recording "The Planets"), and maybe make a timeline showing the earth's progress in space. Students may enjoy creating a space TV story of their own. Using a large roll of butcher paper, divide it into 8-12 frames. Assign a small group of children (2-4) to each frame. Before beginning work on the frames, have the whole group meet together to make up a story and record it. (You may want to add sound effects as well.) Divide the story into 8-12 scenes (measure scene size from the opening size of a cardboard box which will serve as the TV screen later), and draw each scene. When completed, roll up the butcher paper to the opening scene, and pass it across the TV screen as each scene progresses in the narration. (HINT: If you're using a spacecraft throughout the story, make a template for students to trace to keep the size of the craft consistent throughout.)

JUNE IS USUALLY WHEN WE VISIT THE BEACH, so it follows that a unit on the ocean would be timely. After presenting an overview, try making a wax paper lamination (tissue paper adhered to butcher paper using starch) mural of the ocean. Use the mural to show the different levels of the ocean. Set up committees for (1) ocean colors, (2) boats, (3) fish, (4) shells, (5) plants, and (6) the bottom. Use construction paper to make everything except the ocean colors. Remember to change the color as the ocean gets deeper.

JULY

HIGHLIGHTS:

4.....Declaration of Independence

5.....P.T. Barnum born, 1810

7.....World War II begins, 1937

16.....Scientists set off atomic bomb, 1945

19.....First women's rights convention
      in U.S., 1848

30.....Henry Ford born, 1863

EVENTS:

IN JULY, CHILDREN WILL SEE A VARIETY OF BUGS. Collect samples and learn about their life cycles. Butterflies and moths are always good to study. There are many beautiful butterfly coloring books available. You can make butterflies in class. Trace a butterfly shape on two pieces of construction paper. Cut out. Next, cut out spaces for the designs on the wings. Sandwich tissue paper between the two construction paper wings. Staple wings to a tongue depressor, add pipe cleaner antennae, and suspend from the ceiling!

FRUITS AND VEGETABLES are abundant now and can be used in a variety of activities. Of course, discussions can center around food groups and nutrition, but it is also fun to build food sculptures or faces using small food items. Have an English muffin serve as the face, and display a selection of other food items to be used as the features. Another idea is to slice the food exposing a tactile surface with which simple printing can be introduced. With the tempera primary colors of red, blue, and yellow in small containers, create an ABC pattern using the cut food. For example, for "A" use a sliced orange dipped in red, for "B" use a sliced green pepper dipped in yellow, and for "C" use corn on the cob dipped in blue. Let students dip the food into the paint and then print onto the paper in this pattern and repeat it several times to create a beautiful ABC pattern and pattern extension. This will make a lovely display while students learn about color theory.

TAKE A NATURE WALK and adopt a plant for this month. Have students make periodic observations and record data regarding their plant. Draw a picture and make a small report on the plant. Have all the reports put together into a class book on plants from the area.

AUGUST

HIGHLIGHTS:

1.....First census in U.S. completed, 1790
2.....First Lincoln penny issued, 1909
6.....Atomic bomb dropped on
      Hiroshima, 1945
15.....Panama Canal opened, 1914
26 ....Women given the right to vote, 1920

EVENTS:

ON AUGUST 2nd, THE FIRST LINCOLN PENNY was issued. Take 3 pennies, 3 nickels, and 3 nails to use in a scientific experiment. Put one of each of these into its own container of saline solution; soap solution; and as a control group, one in plain water. Observe and record the rate corrosion begins. Plot each group onto a graph or other display. Remember to instruct the children as they progress through the elements in this scientific experiment using a control group, observation, recording data, developing a hypothesis, and theory. (Learning this process is as important as the experiment itself for children.)

MANY PEOPLE GO AWAY ON VACATION THIS MONTH, and as a result, transportation is widely used. Introduce a unit on transportation, or concentrate on automobiles exclusively. Have students design their dream car or make a collage of car pictures. Investigate how a combustible engine works. Build a model engine (working or pretend). Have students plan a trip to another country (travel agencies may help with pamphlets or posters) and have students compute miles. You may even narrow this down to drawing a map of your own neighborhood and plotting mileage to different places. Also, students could research gas mileage per gallon on different cars and decide which would be more economical.

SOLAR GRAPHICS ARE ALWAYS ENJOYABLE. Light sensitive paper can be purchased at photographic supply stores or through science supply catalogs. Items are placed on the paper and left in the sun for differing amounts of time. When finished, the paper is rinsed, and the shadow of the item will print onto the paper. You might like to use this to introduce a unit on cameras and even try making one in the classroom. (Some of the photographic supply companies are open to donating developer and paper for projects if you call them and offer to feature their company in any showings you might have later.)

SEPTEMBER

HIGHLIGHTS:

.....Labor Day (date varies)

17.....Citizenship Day
Constitution Week through September 23, honors
the signing of the U.S. Constitution, 1787

23.....First Day of autumn

26.....Johnny Appleseed born, 1775

27.....American Indian Day honors native Americans

EVENTS:

CELEBRATE THE FIRST DAY OF AUTUMN by making leaf prints in fall colors, or try leaf rubbings using crayons. Discuss the colors of autumn and why the leaves change color. NATURESCOPE magazine has some good examples of leaf experiments for the classroom.

ON JOHNNY APPLESEED DAY, bring in enough apples (various kinds) for everyone. Be sure to have at least three kinds. Put all the apples into a brown bag before students see them. Sitting in a circle, pass the bag around. Before an apple is taken out, ask children to predict which color of apple they will pick. When finished distributing the apples, make a real graph (a graph using actual apples). Talk about which color of apple is largest, smallest, etc. Have the children retrieve their apples and on a piece of paper estimate how many seeds are inside. Cut the apple open (with adult supervision) and find out how accurate their predictions are. Save the seeds. As children taste their apples, list words pertaining to each sense on a chalkboard. For example: taste words, smell words, etc. When finished listing words, pass out a template apple shape for students to trace onto construction paper. Around the outside edge of the tracing, students can copy descriptive words about their apple. Let them glue the seeds in the middle and color. This makes a nice display when mounted onto colored construction paper.

ON AMERICAN INDIAN DAY, bring in information about different Indian stories about the constellations. One American Indian story is about the Big Bear (big dipper) who was shot with a hunter's arrow. As his blood drips down from the heavens, it covers the leaves, and that is why the leaves change color in the fall. There are many similar stories children will enjoy hearing.

OCTOBER

HIGHLIGHTS:

2......Mahatma Ghandi born, 1869
9......Leif Ericson Day (honors early
      Norse explorer of North America)
11......Eleanor Roosevelt born, 1884
12......Columbus Day

16......Noah Webster born, 1758
18......John Adams born, 1735
24......United Nations' Day, 1914
28......Jonas Salk born, 1914
31......Halloween

EVENTS:

LEIF ERICSON, famous for being the first European to set foot on North America, was born in Iceland. He was part of the group of people living in what is now Norway, Denmark, and Sweden. These men built sturdy ships (called dragon ships) and used them to attack sleeping villages. These Northmen, or Norsemen, labeled their style of warfare to "go viking." "Vik" in Norse means "harbor" or "bay," and the word "Vikin" probably came from this root – thus, the Viking Age A.D. 740 to 1050. This culture could serve as a month-long study of the construction of ships, houses, the Runic alphabet, various songs, or important people from that era.

NOAH WEBSTER spent ten years studying the English language and its connection with other languages. Explain etymology or tracing the origins of a word. List interesting words, and let students discover their origins from other languages.

UNITED NATIONS DAY can be celebrated in many ways that promote world peace. Teach children about UNICEF (United Nations International Children's Emergency Fund). They can select a country to represent, dress in that country's costume, or carry their flag and trick-or-treat for the UNICEF fund.

COSTUMES AND DRESSING UP ON HALLOWEEN actually began as a means of frightening away spirits eager to possess the living according to Celtic folklore. It was also the Irish who originated the term jack-o-lantern which comes from another folktale. Jack, a drunk and evil man, tricked the devil into climbing a tree and trapped him by carving a cross on the trunk. Jack kept Satan trapped until he swore he'd never again tempt Jack to sin. Unfortunately, upon his death, Jack found that his reputation prevented him from entering heaven, and unfortunately Satan even refused him entrance into fiery hell. Destined to wander the frigid darkness until Judgment Day, Jack implored the devil for burning embers to light his way. Satan would only part with a single ember, and by putting the ember into a turnip he had chewed hollow, he formed Jack's lantern. (Have your class design and display their lanterns after you share this bit of folklore with them.)

NOVEMBER

HIGHLIGHTS:

 2 .....Daniel Boone born, 1734
 3 .....Robert L. Stevenson born, 1850
11 .....Veteran's Day
24 .....Scott Joplin born, 1868
 .....Thanksgiving, fourth Thursday
 .....Children's Book Week (date varies)

EVENTS:

TO CELEBRATE ROBERT L. STEVENSON'S BIRTHDAY, read several of his poems aloud in class. One excellent source for his poems is *A Child's Garden of Verses*, which is a collection of children's poems. Read, discuss, and illustrate several of the poems for the younger grades. Older grades may enjoy reading from the novel *Kidnapped* or *Treasure Island*. Both these selections can be acted out or used in a puppet presentation.

NOVEMBER 3RD is also the birthday of another important person. John Montagu, the fourth earl of Sandwich, loved gambling more than eating. As the story goes, he once was involved in a card game for over 24 hours straight. To save the time it takes to use a fork, he ordered a piece of meat to be put between two pieces of bread. As a joke, his title Sandwich was given to food served between bread, and the name has stuck! Have students construct their own real or imaginary sandwiches (food drawn on construction paper). Label the parts, and eat or display.

NOVEMBER 16TH is the birthday of W.C. Handy (1873 - 1958), a black band leader and American composer. He was remembered as the "father of the blues." Celebrate this special day by doing hand activities. Give manicures, learn hand signs, trace and color your hands, or walk on your hands. Play handbells, or listen to handbell music. Or, play Handel's *Water Music*.

KING TUT'S TOMB was first uncovered on November 26, 1922. This was one of the most important archeological events in history. King Tut, only 9-years-old when crowned king, died at age 18 and his body was laid to rest in an Egyptian tomb for nearly 3,000 years. Howard Carter, a British archeologist, entered the tomb on this day. It took Carter and his crew ten years to carefully remove the priceless contents of the tomb. Take this time to study the Egyptian culture, King Tut, hieroglyphics (pictures standing for words), etc. Let students design their own form of hieroglyphics or even an original code of their own. Use it to send messages!

DECEMBER

HIGHLIGHTS:

5......Walt Disney born, 1901
8......Eli Whitney born, 1765
10......Human Rights Day
22......First day of winter

24......Kit Carson born, 1809
25......Clara Barton born, 1821
......Christmas Day
31......New Year's Eve
......Hanukkah

EVENTS:

WALT DISNEY (1901-1966) is probably the most important person in the history of animated cartoons. On his birthday, celebrate his perfection of natural movement in cartoon characters by watching some of his own productions. Let students make an animated cartoon book. They can draw a simple picture or stick figure in the same place on each page beginning at the front of the book. Incorporate smaller motions in each page. They can flip the pages to watch their character move.

DECEMBER 22ND IS DESIGNATED AS THE WINTER SOLSTICE, or the first day of winter. On this day, the earth tilts in a way that makes the North Pole as far away from the sun as it can get. This means it is the longest night of the year and the shortest day for the Northern Hemisphere. Talk about hibernation and animals in winter. Include a discussion about the horseshoe hare, whose fur changes to white in winter as a form of self-preservation.

DECEMBER 26 IS CALLED "BOXING DAY" IN ENGLAND. The term "boxing" does not mean fighting but instead refers to the custom of wrapping gifts at Christmas. These boxes were distributed among the public servants and the poor. This year remember all the people who do jobs which help you and your family – mailperson, teachers, class helpers, grocery clerks, etc.

DECEMBER 27TH BEGINS THE AFRO-AMERICAN CELEBRATION OF KWANZA, or first fruits, which lasts seven days, each stressing a different idea: December 26 UMOJA (unity), December 27 KUJICHAGULIA (self-determination), December 28 UJIMA (group effort), December 29 UJAMAA (group economies), December 30 KUUMBA (creativity), December 31 NIA (purpose), January 1 IMANI (faith). The words for each day are in Swahili. Kwazana was started in 1966 by Maulana Ron Karenga and is a celebrated family tradition in many Afro-American homes. Candles in a KINARA candleholder are lit each day of the celebration as the day's theme ideas are discussed. On the last day, gifts are exchanged (ZAWADI) and they share a feast (KARAMU).

ON DECEMBER 29, 1845, TEXAS JOINED THE UNION. Texas at that time was the largest state until Alaska joined in 1959. The popular motto for Texas Admission Day is, "Everything's bigger in Texas!" Try a World's Largest Day celebration by testing your knowledge of the world's records. Name the largest animal, country, ocean, planet in our solar system, plant, building, person, etc.

SUNDAY	MONDAY	TUESDAY	WEDNESDAY	THURSDAY	FRIDAY	SATURDAY